a year in the life of richmond joanna jackson

FRANCES LINCOLN

a year in the life of richmond joanna jackson

To Steve, Ben, Jake and Dylan, the men in my life

Many thanks to: All the staff at Richmond Local Studies
Library, especially Jane Baxter. Their help has been
invaluable. A special thanks to Dick and Steve at Positive
Images. They have been wonderfully helpful with their expert
knowledge and jovial banter. It's a pleasure to do business
with them. Last but not least to Jean at Sandrine Chocolates
for all her support and encouragement.

Frances Lincoln Limited
4 Torriano Mews
Torriano Avenue
London NW5 2RZ

A Year in the Life of Richmond
Copyright © Frances Lincoln Limited 2005

Text and photographs copyright © Joanna Jackson 2005

First Frances Lincoln edition 2005

British Library Cataloguing-in-Publication Data
A catalogue record for this book is available from
the British Library.

ISBN 0-7112-2526-5

Printed in Singapore by Star Standard

9 8 7 6 5 4 3 2 1

contents

Introduction   6

winter   8
Shene Manor   10
The view   14
The green   22
Architecture   26

spring   32
The Tudors in Richmond   40
The Royal Star & Garter Home   44
Almshouses   48
The Georgian era   52

summer   58
The river   62
Bridges   70
Music   76
Pubs   80

autumn   84
Rugby   90
The Poppy Factory   96
The park   100
Theatres   104

Index   112

Rather chilly for boating:
rowing boats wait for
warmer days.

introduction

Over the years Richmond has evolved into the wonderful place it is today. There have been three main influences on that development: the river, the railway and the patronage of various royal families through the ages.

The town's recorded history goes back to the middle of the tenth century. It was originally a hamlet or small village with a cluster of fishermen's cottages and a simple manor house. It has been said that Edward the Confessor, 'delighting in the fair scenery', called the tiny hamlet by the Thames 'Syenes'. At the time of the Domesday survey, Syene or Shene, as it was formally known, was part of a royal manor, the Anglo-Saxon kings' town that is now, of course, known as Kingston. The name Shene probably came from either the Anglo-Saxon word sceo, meaning 'shelter', or sciene, meaning 'shining'. In 1501 Henry VII changed the name to Rychmonde, after his earldom in Yorkshire, but Shene still exists today as East Sheen, one mile east of Richmond on the present South Circular road.

It was the plentiful supply of fish in the river that must have seduced the first people to settle here, providing a source of food and income. The beautiful situation, beside the river and below the hill, attracted the first royals. Whenever a royal party descended on the place to stay at the manor house or, later, the palace, a huge retinue of servants and hangers-on accompanied them and all had to be accommodated. It was stated by one chronicler, called Stow, in the Annals of the time, that one particularly extravagant Queen, Anne of Bohemia, had ten thousand guests dining at the king's table every day. Even assuming this was a gross exaggeration there must have been a very large number of people staying in the area. Many houses were built for royal servants and guests, and large numbers of inns sprung up to take care of any overflow. Highly skilled carpenters and builders, dressmakers, blacksmiths, brewers, cooks and entertainers all came to Richmond to find work, and ended up settling here. Later, rich merchants, writers and artists built grand second homes, often travelling to and from their city dwelling by boat along the river.

In 1846 the first railway line reached Richmond. The London and South Western Railway from Nine Elms in Battersea to Richmond was formally opened in July of that year, providing seventeen trains daily in both directions. This line was extended to Waterloo and Datchet in 1848, and to Windsor in 1849. The District Line, originally the Kensington and Richmond Railway, was opened in January 1869. The coming of the railways had a profound effect on the town, nearly doubling the population from 10,962 in 1861 to 19,066 in 1889. Richmond had become a middle-class haven for well-heeled commuters.

Richmond has always thrived on service industries and tourism, rather than on manufacturing. This is as true today as it was in 1501. The town is full of restaurants, pubs and shops (the big chains in the high street as well as many interesting, independently owned little places found down countless alleys). These amenities, together with the wonderful location, make Richmond a fabulous place to live in and visit alike.

winter

shene manor

Feudal England was divided into counties, the counties into hundreds and the hundreds into manors. Each of these had its own manor house, residence of the local lord of the manor. It is believed that Kingston's manor house was situated by the river at Shene. In the period of the Saxon and Viking kings Kingston had great political importance. No fewer than seven Anglo-Saxon kings were crowned at the Kings' Stone between 900 and 979. This historical stone can still be found in Kingston, near the town hall.

The domain of Shene was split into upper and lower fields, which were further divided into shots (a distance roughly the length of a bowshot). Parkshot, the home today of an adult education centre, retains its name from these times. It is recorded that Henry I (1068–1135) rented the manor house to the influential Belot family. The estate was leased out for about two centuries and first king to make use of it was Edward II (1284–1327).

Edward was a Plantagenet, the youngest child and only surviving son (though he had at least twelve sisters) of Edward I, nicknamed Edward Longshanks (1239–1307), and his first wife, Eleanor of Castile. Edward was the first son of an English king to be created Prince of Wales, and it was as Prince of Wales that he first came to Shene.

Edward became king on the death of his father in 1307, and in the following year he married Isabella, the twelve-year-old daughter of Philippe IV of France. In 1314 Edward and his English army were soundly beaten by the Scots at the Battle of Bannockburn. As Edward fled from Robert the Bruce, he vowed that if he escaped he would found a monastery for the Carmelites. He did escape and kept his word, building a monastery in Richmond.

Throughout his reign Edward was surrounded by foolish counsellors and beset by war abroad and rebellion at home, and in 1327 he was forced to abdicate in favour of his fourteen-year-old son. Early in his reign the boy king Edward III (1312–77) formally granted the manor of Shene to his mother, Queen Isabella, to live in for the rest of her life. For the next few years it was Isabella and her lover, Roger Mortimer, who really governed the country, but an older Edward exerted his power. Shortly before his eighteenth birthday he had Mortimer arrested and issued a proclamation announcing that he had taken the government of the realm into his own hands.

After Isabella's death in 1358 Edward took over Shene and developed the house into a palace fit for a king. He used it a great deal during the latter part of his reign and died there on 22 June 1377.

Edward's grandson Richard II (1367–1400), who succeeded him, also lived for long periods at the palace at Shene. At the age of fifteen Richard married Anne of Bohemia, daughter of the Emperor Charles IV. The couple became devoted to each other, and Shene of all the royal residences was their favourite place to stay. They built a summerhouse on one of the islands in the Thames as a romantic retreat away from affairs of state.

Richard and Anne entertained lavishly at Shene, and more and more houses were built in the area to accommodate the huge numbers of court visitors. During this time Geoffrey Chaucer became Clerk of Works for the King and was a regular visitor to Shene.

It was at Shene that, in 1394, Queen Anne died of the plague. Richard, distraught at her death, ordered the

PREVIOUS PAGE Old Father Thames braves winter in Terrace Gardens.

BELOW Cholmondeley Walk early one winter's morning.

demolition of the palace and all its surrounding buildings. It appears from local records that the King's orders were not carried out to their full extent, as agricultural buildings and the gardens continued to be maintained. However, the main building was left derelict for many years.

On his accession to the throne in 1413, Henry V (1387–1422) brought the court back to Shene and rebuilt the palace so that it was better and more splendid than before. He also implemented an unfulfilled promise of his father, Henry IV (1367–1413), to found three religious houses, building them in the Shene area. One, a Carthusian monastery known as the Charterhouse of Jesus of Bethlehem in Shene, became the largest and richest of all the English charterhouses. It was built on the site now occupied by the Royal Mid-Surrey Golf Club. A miniature replica is to be found in Richmond's museum.

Little of historical note happened after this in Shene for many years, until the reign of Henry VII. Then, in 1497, there was a disastrous fire that destroyed large parts of the old palace. The King began a radical programme of reconstruction. It was at this time that Shene was renamed Richmond, and its glory days under the Tudor dynasty began.

Railings flank the bridge
leading from the towpath
to the Old Deer Park.

the view

TOP The path to the river from Richmond Hill.

BOTTOM, LEFT Early-morning frost lies on Petersham Meadow.

BOTTOM, RIGHT The Thames Valley from Richmond Hill, with the Petersham Hotel in the foreground.

The view from the top of Richmond Hill has inspired composers, poets, playwrights and artists for the last four hundred years. It is the only view in England that is protected by law. A special Act of Parliament was passed in 1902 to protect the hill setting and view, which at that time was under attack by a local property developer.

Four centuries before, another property speculator, Michael Pew, had seen the potential of the site. At the end of the seventeenth century he constructed three substantial houses and in front of them built The Terrace, 10 yards wide and 100 yards long and bordered on both sides by trees. This walk is as popular today as it was then. The Roebuck, built next to Pew's houses in about 1715, still remains and serves drinks on balmy summer evenings to the crowds watching the sun go down over the Thames Valley below.

By the late eighteenth century the hill had become a most fashionable place to live. Sir Joshua Reynolds had Wick House built as a country retreat and Thomas Gainsborough lived opposite, at 2 The Terrace. Turner resided in nearby Twickenham, coming regularly to paint the view. Two paintings of the vista, *Richmond Hill on the Prince Regent's Birthday*, by Turner, and *The Thames from Richmond Hill*, by Reynolds, hang in Tate Britain today.

At the end of The Terrace is Nightingale Lane. In 1820 Wordsworth wrote a poem about the beautiful birdsong to be heard there:

> For I have heard the quire of Richmond Hill
> Chanting with indefatigable bill . . .

Sadly the nightingale no longer sings in Nightingale Lane.

In the late seventeenth century, the composer Henry Purcell was moved to write the song 'On the brow of Richmond Hill':

> On the brow of Richmond Hill
> Which Europe scarce can parallel
> Ev'ry eye such wonders fill
> To view the prospect round.
> Where the silver Thames doth glide
> And stately courts are edified
> Meadows decked in summer pride
> With verdant beauties crowned . . .

James Thomson was the first poet to immortalize the view from Richmond Hill, in 'Seasons'. A Richmond resident, he was however more famous for writing the words, in 1740, to 'Rule, Britannia'. (This was very generous of him, considering that he was Scottish and the Union was at that time still widely unpopular north of the border.)

Downe House, further along The Terrace, was the home in the late eighteenth century of Richard Sheridan who wrote *School for Scandal* while he was living there.

At the present time the view is in a state of transition. The centenary of the Act of Protection was celebrated in 2002 and a group of interested locals launched the Arcadia Initiative. The intention is to work with English Heritage and the Thames Landscape Strategy body to preserve the view and try to restore it to its even more splendid past by removing trees that have grown so large that they block out some of the original vista.

The view from Richmond Hill, shrouded in winter fog.

LEFT A winter sun rises over
the Old Deer Park.

BELOW Obelisks in the Old
Deer Park, once used by
astronomers to establish due
south from the observatory.

LEFT Terrace Gardens in fog.

ABOVE The frosted skeleton of a leaf.

the green

OPPOSITE, TOP
Victorian architecture
in Portland Terrace.

OPPOSITE, BOTTOM
Pembroke Villas
look down over the
snowy green.

Richmond's green began its life as a rough field in front of the original manor house. As early as the thirteenth century, Edward I and Eleanor of Castile held tourneys on this piece of land when visiting the manor at Shene.

A tourney, which consisted of ritualized combat between parties of knights, provided a good excuse for lots of pageantry and much overeating and drinking. These events were always full of pomp and ceremony. The royal party sat on a raised platform erected outside the gates of the manor house while the knights rode past in full armour, preceded by pages carrying their personal standards aloft. In the bouts horses as well as the knights had to be protected with armour from the blunt swords or heavy wooden maces wielded. In the jousting contests, contestants bearing long lances would charge at each other. The aim in both events was not to harm one's opponent but only to unseat him from his horse. However, accidents happened, old scores were paid off and combatants often died.

Henry VIII held many tourneys at Richmond and court records relate expenses, 'for velvets and silks and for embroiderers and saddlers provided for the jousts at Richmond £446 10s 9½d'. The velvets and silks were awarded to the winners of the bouts.

By the reign of Elizabeth I tourneys were rare, but when the Queen was in residence the green expanse was used for pageants and other spectacles. Bull and bear baiting were favourite sports with ordinary folk as well as the nobility, and wagers on the outcome were common.

During the daytime sheep were pastured on this common ground. There were complaints to the Richmond vestry (an early law-and-order body) about domestic animals being allowed to roam at will and wealthier occupants of local houses began to grumble, annoyed by the 'stench of the dung of hogs and cattle'. These offences are found throughout vestry records of the seventeenth and eighteenth centuries. Fines were administered to the guilty parties.

There were only a few houses around the green in Elizabethan times, but by the eighteenth century many more had been built in the Queen Anne and Georgian styles. These houses still exist, particularly around the southeast corner of the green. They are Grade I listed and of great architectural significance.

Cricket has been played on the green since at least 1666 when Sir Robert Paston wrote to his wife, 'Post now comes from the Squire of the Body who says he saw your son very well engaged in a game at criquett on Richmond Green.' In 1731 history was made when a match between two aristocratic teams ended in a draw – the first time a draw had ever been recorded. Cricket is still played every week through the summer and after the match the players take a drink or two in the Cricketers pub. One of the oldest pubs in Richmond, in the eighteenth century it was known as the Crickett Players. Cricket then was played for money, and considerable sums changed hands in wagers.

The May Fair, now a regular fixture, was started in 1970 with a few stalls around Richmond parish church. Today the whole of the green is needed for stalls and entertainments. Hundreds of people turn up for the event, and it almost invariably rains.

Today the green is as popular as ever. On summer evenings it is packed with people playing games, picnicking or lying on the grass having a drink in beautiful surroundings.

OPPOSITE, TOP The neo-
Georgian development
on the riverfront.

OPPOSITE, BOTTOM Winter
reveals the skeletons of
trees on Richmond Green.

ABOVE Looking across
the green towards
Pembroke Villas.

architecture

TOP Old Palace Terrace is a fine example of a Georgian terrace.

BOTTOM The neo-gothic architecture of the American University.

Richmond is a fine example of a Georgian town. The area around the southwest corner of the green is of particular importance, with Old Palace Lane and Maids of Honour Row both composed of Grade 1 listed buildings. However, many other architectural styles are also represented in buildings dotted around the area.

Little survives from Tudor days but a small part of the palace and a couple of houses, now greatly modified, in George Street. Tudor architecture is noteworthy for its brickwork, which was often decorative with wooden struts providing structural support. People who could not afford bricks used plaster and painted it white, producing the characteristic black-and-white style. In the Tudor era chimneys and fireplaces became common for the first time.

The Georgian kings had a huge influence on Richmond. The royal court brought members of the aristocracy as well as wealthy merchants and businessmen to the area. By then the Grand Tour had become fashionable and rich young men were travelling around Europe, visiting in particular Greece and Italy – the Georgian equivalent of the Gap Year. The experiences of these young men were reflected in the architecture of the period. Palladianism was a philosophy of design based on the writings and work of Andrea Palladio, an Italian architect of the sixteenth century who tried to recreate the style of the buildings of Ancient Rome.

Georgian architecture is characterized by its terraces. Walls between houses were built extra thick to prevent the spread of fire. Roofs were hidden behind parapets, door cases had fanlights and pillars were used in porches. Marshgate House and Wick House are fine examples of the style. The Georgians were also partial to follies, grottoes and bridges in their gardens and both Terrace Gardens and Marble Hill Park have grottoes.

The Victorians flooded into Richmond when the railways arrived and commuting became a way of life. Once again the green provides the setting for good examples of housing, this time the Victorian architecture in Pembroke Villas and Portland Terrace on the northwest and southeast sides.

The neo-gothic style became very popular during this era. More a spiritual than an architectural movement, it was a reaction to the mass-produced monotony of the Industrial Revolution. The style of Horace Walpole's neo-gothic house, Strawberry Hill, was copied in Richmond in 1843 by the Methodists, who built a teaching institution at the top of the hill (now the American University). Ellecker House (now the Old Vicarage School), was converted to the neo-gothic style in 1809, and Gothic House on the green is also an example of the trend. All these buildings have strong vertical lines, pointed window and door frames, and buttressed walls and parapets. The influence of this style can also be seen in the bay windows and porches of smaller houses.

During the 1920s and 1930s the Art Deco movement flourished, influenced by Cubism and the art of the Ancient Egyptian, Aztec and Mayan civilizations. The Poppy Factory, the Odeon cinema on the hill and the railway station are all examples of this type of architecture.

The 1960s provided us with some hideous buildings, and Quinlan Terry's neo-Georgian riverfront caused controversy in the 1980s. Prince Charles backed the architect for using a style that was sympathetic to its surroundings, but other architects called for a more progressive design.

Christmas lights sparkle
in Paved Court.

A snowman guards the
way in Queen's Ride,
Richmond Park.

A splendid red deer stag
surveys his territory in
Richmond Park.

spring

PREVIOUS PAGE Old Father
Thames in spring
sunshine.

BELOW, LEFT A riot of
colour in the Isabella
Plantation.

BELOW, RIGHT Glorious
spring flowers: azalea
(*top*) and rhododendron
(*bottom*).

LEFT Magnolia buds
bursting into flower in
Terrace Gardens.

BELOW The vista through
Terrace Gardens to
the river.

Daffodils in parks and
gardens herald the arrival
of spring in Richmond.

the tudors in richmond

Henry Tudor (1457–1509) returned from exile in France to fight against Richard III (1452–85) in the Wars of the Roses. By winning the Battle of Bosworth Field and marrying Elizabeth of York, he united the red and white roses of the houses of Lancaster and York and initiated the great Tudor dynasty. Henry established his court at Shene Palace.

At Christmas 1497 the royal entourage was gathered at Shene when a devastating fire occurred that destroyed the building, and, according to accounts of the time, nearly took the lives of the King and Queen. Henry VII loved Shene and, although generally regarded as a stingy man, he spared no expense in rebuilding it. He named the magnificent new palace Rychmonde after his earldom in Richmond, Yorkshire.

It was at Richmond that the marriages were celebrated of Henry's daughter Margaret to James, King of Scotland, and of his son Arthur, Prince of Wales, to Catherine of Aragon. The latter marriage lasted only five months before the young prince died of the plague. His widow was allotted rooms in the palace, which continued as her main residence, and she was betrothed to Arthur's younger brother, Henry.

Henry VII died in Richmond Palace in 1509. His body lay in state for three days before being taken for burial at Westminster Abbey. His son (1491–1547) became Henry VIII, and seven weeks after his father's death he married Catherine of Aragon.

Henry was strongly built, good at sports, acting and music, and loved entertaining. There was a tennis court at Richmond, and many tourneys were held on the open land outside the palace. On New Year's Day 1510 Catherine gave birth to a son at Richmond Palace. There were great celebrations but unfortunately the baby died after seven weeks. Poor Catherine had eight further children of whom only one, the future 'Bloody' Queen Mary (1516–58), survived infancy.

In fact Henry already had a son, the illegitimate child of one of the Queen's waiting women, and the boy, Henry Fitzroy, was created Duke of Richmond at the age of six. When no legitimate son was forthcoming, however, Henry turned his attentions to Anne Boleyn. The Queen was often left at Richmond with the young princess while Henry enjoyed himself elsewhere.

At this time Cardinal Wolsey was building himself a palace just up the river at Hampton Court. Henry became increasingly jealous of his cardinal's fabulous new residence. Wolsey prudently offered to swap properties with the King, and he moved to Richmond while Henry relocated to Hampton Court. After Wolsey's death Richmond Palace became the place of exile for Henry's now ex-wife, Catherine.

After the short marriage to Anne Boleyn that produced the future Queen Elizabeth (1533–1603), Henry married Jane Seymour. She died at Richmond Palace two weeks after giving birth to a son, Edward (1537–53). Henry's fourth wife was Anne of Cleves, nicknamed the Flanders Mare. This marriage was never consummated and Anne was left to live at Richmond after her divorce. Henry did, however, continue to visit her, often coming down the river from Hampton Court.

When Henry died his frail young son became king. Edward VI loved Richmond and was going to make it his permanent home, but he died at the age of sixteen. His half-sister Queen Mary then ruled for five unhappy, turbulent years before being succeeded by the young Elizabeth I.

Richmond was often awash with dignitaries. The King of France came to woo Elizabeth, and the defence of the realm against the Spanish Armada was planned at Richmond. There are nine recorded occasions on which William Shakespeare's theatre troupe performed here.

The most compact and easy to heat of the royal residences, the palace became known as the Winter Box. During Elizabeth's reign lead pipes were installed to bring water from conduits on Richmond Hill and, almost certainly, one of the first flushing lavatories was fitted here. John Harrington, the inventor of the appliance, was the Queen's godson.

Elizabeth died in the palace on 24 March 1603, probably in the room known as the Queen's Room. History records that from the window of this narrow apartment over the palace archway Lady Scrope dropped the Blue Ring, a sapphire ring belonging to James VI of Scotland, to her brother, Sir Robert Carey. The ring was taken to Edinburgh and given to James to signal that the Queen was dead and he was now King of England as well as Scotland.

The glory years of Richmond died with Elizabeth, and the palace became a residence of royal children rather than that of the sovereign. James' son Henry, the Prince of Wales, lived and died at Richmond, building an art gallery there. Charles I occasionally took up residence, to avoid the plague in London and to enjoy the hunting in nearby Richmond Park, which he enclosed solely for that purpose. After Charles' execution the Commonwealth ordered the palace to be stripped and it began to fall into disrepair.

The era of the Tudors, however, had seen Richmond grow immensely in size and wealth, and set it well on its way to being the town it is today.

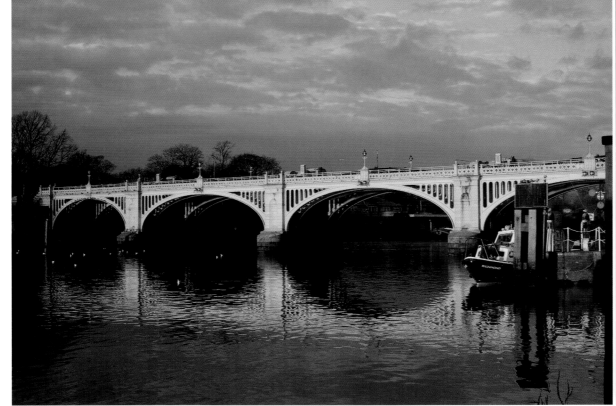

LEFT, TOP A journey to work along the towpath.

LEFT, BOTTOM Spring sunshine lights up the pedestrian bridge by the lock.

RIGHT A heron watches the sun set behind the river.

the royal star & garter home

There has been an inn by the name of the Star and Garter in Richmond since Henry VIII's reign and since 1738 it has been situated in a prime position at the top of Richmond Hill, overlooking the famous view. The original inn was just an alehouse but when the owner, John Christopher, died his two sons built a three-storey hotel next door.

In 1801 James Brewer acquired the buildings and enlarged them considerably, constructing a grand ballroom where the rich and famous of the day came to party. However, he overstretched his spending, went bankrupt and died a broken man in debtors' prison in 1808.

Christopher Crean, the former cook to the Duke of York, reopened the hotel and entertained such illustrious visitors to the country as Tsar Alexander of Russia and King Frederick William of Prussia. Charles Dickens was a regular guest. He would hold a large banquet annually to celebrate his

wedding anniversary and he used the hotel to launch *David Copperfield*.

In 1870 a large fire engulfed the building and destroyed all the older parts. It was rebuilt two years later in a rather grand Italian Romanesque style. However, the hotel fell from favour at the turn of the century and closed in 1906.

At the start of the First World War the Star and Garter took on a new role. It was recognized that there was no provision for soldiers returning from the front with severe injuries and Queen Mary instructed the Red Cross to search for a suitable building in which to look after some of these men. The hotel was purchased for this purpose and 14 January 1916 saw the admittance of its first sixty-five patients. Their average age was just twenty.

Ten masseuses, the forerunners to modern-day physiotherapists, were employed to provide massages, exercises and electrotherapy, and the Star and Garter became one of the first rehabilitation units. In the first year, five young men were sufficiently rehabilitated to leave the home and return to civilian life. Occupational therapy was introduced and crafts were taught to help give the men a sense of purpose. The old hotel required an expensive conversion to make it suitable for its new function and a campaign was started to raise money. One fundraising event encouraged children to donate a penny each and 5.5 million children gave money. The newly refurbished Star and Garter Home was opened by George V and Queen Mary in 1924.

A specialist paraplegic ward was set up after the Second World War under the direction of the eminent Dr Ludwig Guttmann. An expert in the treatment of spinal injuries, he also set up the world-famous Stoke Mandeville Hospital.

OPPOSITE The grand building, in Italian Romanesque style, of the Royal Star & Garter Home.

BELOW Sunrise over the Royal Star & Garter Home.

When the first paraplegic games took place in 1948, they included an archery competition between teams from the Star and Garter and Stoke Mandeville.

The home gained royal status in 1979, with Elizabeth II as its patron, and today is known as the Royal Star & Garter. At the time of writing, however, its future is in limbo. The building is once again considered unsuitable for the needs of its patients and three purpose-built regional centres are planned to care for the ex-servicemen. Although no one knows what will happen to the building, it will surely live on – if only because of its magnificent position looking down over the most painted view in England.

ABOVE Hill Rise is full of fascinating shops, restaurants and pubs.

OPPOSITE Details of two houses on Hill Rise.

almshouses

The poor were always quite well cared for in Richmond. Official poor relief came in the shape of a workhouse set up in 1729, but there is also a long history of private citizens providing charity in the form of money, food or clothing. The most generous form of gift came in the provision of almshouses. Richmond's prosperous past is reflected in the number of almshouses endowed for its poor residents. This accommodation is still in existence today, inhabited by long-term residents of the parish who have no savings or property of their own to support them.

The first almshouses in Richmond were built in 1600 by Sir George Wright to accommodate eight poor aged women. Later, more houses were added and the development became known as Queen Elizabeth's Almshouses. The buildings were originally situated on the Petersham Road but they fell into disrepair and were rebuilt in their present location in the Vineyard in 1767.

Bishop Duppa's Almshouses were built in the 1660s. Before the Civil War, Bishop Duppa lived in Richmond as tutor to the young Charles, Prince of Wales, later to be Charles II. He remained in Richmond throughout the period of the Commonwealth and, although he was a known Royalist and his house was raided on more than one occasion, he managed to survive that turbulent time. He is said to have vowed to establish almshouses if he retained his head and his royal pupil was restored to the throne. He did keep his head and his former charge did become king, so Bishop Duppa, as good as his word, endowed almshouses at Richmond for ten unmarried women over the age of fifty.

In 1695 Humphrey Michel founded almshouses for ten married or single men. In 1757 Rebecca Houblon, who with her sister later became famous for closing down the debauched Richmond Wells, set up almshouses for nine single women. The almshouses remain in all their original glory in Worple Way. Further down Sheen Road are the Church Estate and Hickey's Almshouses. William Hickey was a wealthy resident who founded a trust in 1727 to provide a pension for six men and ten women. The endowed property, which provided an income for the trust, became increasingly valuable and the trustees decided to use the profits to build almshouses, constructing twenty homes for ten men and ten women. This trust is still expanding, twenty-nine units having been added over the years. The Church Estate Almshouses are next to Hickey's, and have also expanded as funds in the trust multiplied.

As well as being given a roof over their heads, the poor men and women were provided for in other ways. Nearly all were given a monthly payment, an annual provision of coal, a cloak or greatcoat every other year, and the attention of a nurse or other medical help if necessary.

There were, however, strings attached. At Michel's Almshouses, for instance, 'Any person that shall keep disorderly hours or at any time be found drunk shall for the first offence forfeit 4d, for the second 8d and for the 3rd 1s and after admonition, if he do not amend shall be expelled from the house.' Inmates were also fined for 'begging, breaking hedges or stealing wood'. Beneficiaries of the Houblon sisters had to be able to recite the Lord's Prayer, the Apostles' Creed and the Ten Commandments, and they had also to have lived a virtuous, sober and honest life.

Still, perhaps this was a small price to pay for the security of knowing you would be looked after in your declining years.

BELOW, CLOCKWISE FROM TOP
Roses scramble along the
wall of Bishop Duppa's
Almshouses; the neat
frontage of the Church
Estate Almshouses; an
imposing arch gives on
to Hickey's Almshouses.

OVERLEAF Blossom weighs
down the branches of
cherry trees along the
Great Chertsey Road and
in the Old Deer Park.

the georgian era

CLOCKWISE FROM TOP LEFT
This little alley has been known as Brewers Lane since 1608; Asgill House, built in 1757 for Sir Charles Asgill, Lord Mayor of London; Marshgate House, a fine example of Georgian architecture; 3 The Terrace, home of Mrs Fitzherbert, mistress of George IV; a typical Georgian window.

The Hanoverian dynasty began in 1714 with the arrival of George I (1660–1727). He was brought over from Germany following the death of Queen Anne (1665–1714), who had no surviving children. An elderly and unprepossessing man who could speak very little English, he was considered by the Whig government of the day to be preferable to the Stuart alternative. Because of his lack of English the cabinet appointed one of its members to oversee all proceedings. This was the first Prime Minister, Sir Robert Walpole.

The Georgian kings were, with the exception of George III, a pretty debauched lot. They had numerous mistresses and universally the sons and fathers couldn't stand each other. These factors were to have quite a profound influence on the development of the Richmond area.

George's son, another George (1683–1760), became Prince of Wales when his father acceded to the throne. He and his wife, Caroline of Ansbach, hated living in the same house as the grumpy king and spent much time at Richmond Lodge. This mansion stood on the site of what is now the Old Deer Park. It was originally built in the sixteenth century by Dean Colet, founder of St Paul's School, and was later enlarged by the Earl of Ormonde, a Jacobean and supporter of the Stuart dynasty. Ormonde's estates were confiscated by the crown because of his affinity with the Catholics and the lodge was sold to the Prince of Wales for £6,000. George and Caroline were a fashionable couple and their set flocked to Richmond.

In 1727 the Prince of Wales became George II. Like his father before him, he kept numerous mistresses. He built Marble Hill House in Twickenham for Henrietta Howard, one of his many muses. Maids of Honour Row, the beautiful collection of Georgian houses on Richmond Green, was built to accommodate Caroline's maids of honour.

Sir Robert Walpole, the Prime Minister, came regularly to Richmond and struck up a friendship with Caroline. An astute woman, she became very influential and in many ways had more power than her husband over the policy of the time. She was also greatly extravagant, creating whimsical follies such as a grotto filled with waxwork images. Her loyal Prime Minister dealt with her bills. (As a side-issue, she also caused much local gossip by having an affair with Stephen Duck, one of her garden labourers.)

George II and Caroline carried on the family tradition by loathing their eldest son, Frederick. Frederick and his wife, Augusta, set up a rival court at Kew. Frederick died before becoming king but Augusta stayed in Kew, bringing up her family and at the same time enlarging and improving the grounds around the house.

George III (1738–1820), Frederick's oldest son, was very different from his grandfather and great-grandfather and from his siblings, who all turned out wild after a strict upbringing at Kew. A simple soul who loved agriculture, he was nicknamed 'Farmer George'. He married Charlotte Sophia of Mecklenburg-Strelitz. They were happily married for years until he was overtaken by the hereditary disease of porphyria, and began to suffer from prolonged bouts of insanity.

George and Charlotte lived in Richmond Lodge during the summer. The increasing size of his family (he was to end up with fifteen children), led the King to plan the enlargement of the house and he sought to purchase more land from the local Vestry. They refused to sell and a furious George III left the Lodge in a huff, moving his family back to Kew. His wife

BELOW A lovely Georgian house in The Wick.

OPPOSITE Listed buildings and cherry blossom in Maids of Honour Row, a superb Georgian terrace.

loved the garden at Kew and continued the work of her mother-in-law, improving and enlarging the area. The result is the Botanical Gardens, a World Heritage Site and a magnificent legacy to have left the country. The cottage that Charlotte built in the grounds still exists today.

Farmer George had a ha-ha, or ditch, dug alongside the towpath between Richmond and Kew to keep his cattle from straying. It is still there now, providing a sanctuary for many ducks and other wildlife. George was interested in astronomy, and he built an observatory in the gardens at Richmond Lodge. This also survives, now sited in the middle of the Royal Mid-Surrey golf course. The observatory was built in 1769 specifically for the purpose of viewing the transit of Venus across the sun in June of that year. The Hanoverian Herschel was appointed as George's astronomer. Two obelisks in the Old Deer Park were erected to line up with the telescope to show the position of due south. Before the observatory was built at Greenwich, the calculations made here helped set London's official time for many years.

George and Charlotte's oldest son, yet another George (1762–1830), was naturally disliked by his father and, like his forebears, he was a womanizer. When he was only twenty, he used to smuggle the renowned beauty Mrs Robinson ('Perdita') through the garden gate into his apartments at Kew. There was, however, one woman who would not become his mistress. She was Mrs Fitzherbert, a devout Catholic with strict morals. There were three Acts of Parliament barring anyone married to a Catholic from succeeding to the throne. Nevertheless George married her, though in the strictest secrecy. Married in 1785, by the Vicar of Twickenham, they spent the honeymoon at Mrs Fitzherbert's house, No. 3 The

Terrace, on the top of Richmond Hill. George later moved his bride to Marble Hill House. In 1795, however, he was constrained to undertake a marriage of convenience with his cousin Caroline of Brunswick.

The Georgians' reign of just over a hundred years influenced Richmond considerably. The high street is named George Street, in recognition of the benefits brought to the town by the royal presence. Many of the Georgian houses survive in all their glory, and of course the wonderful Kew Gardens remains on our doorstep.

Children enjoy all the fun
of Richmond's May Fair.

summer

PREVIOUS PAGE Old Father Thames surrounded by summer foliage.

RIGHT Haymaking in Richmond Park.

the river

The river has played a hugely important role in the evolution of the town of Richmond upon Thames. No doubt the original inhabitants elected to live next to the river because it provided a ready supply of food and water, as well as a transport route. Many market gardens grew up in the country around Richmond and Hampton, and London's women 'coddlers' travelled to the area in the pea-gathering season to look for work. The produce – green vegetables, potatoes and fruit – was taken back to London on sailing barges, piled high in wicker baskets ready for market. For the wealthier members of society, however, it was the beauty of the riverside that was Richmond's main attraction.

One of the most common occupations of Richmond's working class was that of waterman. The watermen were the equivalent of today's taxi drivers. Their taxi was their wherry, a rowing boat that would take you either across the river or further afield. Up until 1514 the fare was bargained for, but during the reign of Henry VIII fixed charges were established.

Records of royal expenses incurred at Richmond during Tudor times suggest that the river provided the main highway between Richmond and London. It took three hours on the tide to reach the City of London with one man rowing, but only two hours if the passenger paid double fare and a second oarsman joined the crew. Elizabeth I had her own royal barge with two cabins and ornamental glass windows, painted with elaborate designs and gilding. Twenty-one watermen rowed her to Richmond.

By the eighteenth century the watermen had formed a co-operative and profits were shared out every Saturday night at the White Cross Inn. There were three piers at the quay in the town centre and two ferries, one for foot passengers and one a horse ferry. The latter was a large platform for carrying horses and carts; carriages still had to go all the way to the bridge at Kingston to cross the river.

Many rowing races took place on the river, with the watermen competing against each other. Much gambling accompanied these races and a great deal of money changed hands. The most famous race, an annual event, was the Doggett's Coat and Badge, started in 1715 to mark the first anniversary of George I's accession to the throne. It continues to this day and is now the longest-running sporting event in the world.

The river police were established in 1798, initially to reduce theft from cargoes in the Port of London. By 1839 they patrolled an area from Deptford to Teddington. The police boat was a forty-foot double-scull galley with a crew of five – two men to row, two to watch and one inspector.

The Thames was originally a good source of fish and in the *Gentleman's Magazine* of 1749 it was reported, 'Two of the greatest known draughts of salmon were caught in the Thames below Richmond that have been known for some years. One net having 35 large salmon in it and the other 22 which lowered the price of fresh salmon at Billingsgate from 1/-s to 6d per pound.' In 1769 a sturgeon six feet in length was caught and presented to the King.

Less than a hundred years later the fish had gone and the Thames was so revoltingly polluted that it was considered a dead river. This situation lasted for over a hundred years. Cholera epidemics due to unclean water were common in London throughout the Victorian era. In the summer of 1858, the Big Stink occurred, when the combination of unusually

hot weather and a river full of sewage made it necessary to hang sacking soaked in deodorizing chemicals at the windows of the House of Commons.

This unpleasant working environment quickly focused the minds of the politicians and the construction of London's sewer system was begun. In the twentieth century efforts to clean up the Thames continued. By 1963 eels had reappeared and, by the year 2000, 118 species of fish had returned to the river. A seal was spotted fishing by Richmond Bridge in 1986 and salmon are back – a testament to the cleanness of the water now.

There are many swans on the river. Those at Richmond belong to the Crown or to either the Vintners' Company or the Dyers' Company (two livery companies of the City of London). Legend has it that swans were originally introduced to this country by Richard the Lionheart, who picked them up in Cyprus on his way back from the crusades in the late twelfth century. Each year in July the ceremony of swan upping is conducted on the river between London and Henley. The Queen's Keeper of the Swans and the swan masters, representatives of the two companies, row from Tower Pier to Henley, identifying and marking the year-old cygnets belonging to the companies. The swans belonging to the Crown remain unmarked.

Richmond was always a popular place to visit and a gentle stroll by the river was one of the distractions that drew the visitors. Until the middle of the eighteenth century the only walk led past the site of the old palace. This was called Cholmondeley Walk after the Earl of Cholmondeley, who lived in a house on the site now occupied by Maids of Honour Row. An Act of Parliament in 1777 authorized the building of a new towpath from Kew to Water Lane. The new path, which was later extended to Ham, made a stroll along the river even more attractive to the fashionable set of the day and increased the number of visitors, some of whom liked the area so much that they bought houses in the locality. The watermen and boat builders flourished as huge fleets of rowing boats were built for hire and entertainments such as races and regattas became common.

When the river froze people could sometimes skate over it and during a couple of exceptionally cold winters the ice was thick enough for a fair to be held on top. Before the nineteenth century two factors combined to slow down the flow of the river, making it easier for ice to form. One was the greater width of the river (the concrete embankment had not yet been built) and the other the thickness of the pillars of the old London Bridge. Even so, the weather must have been pretty chilly. In 1739 the river froze from 25 December until 17 February and in 1788 the river was again frozen for several weeks. The frost fairs were special events: stalls were put up, oxen were roasted and fireworks were set off. The icing over ceased after the new London Bridge was built in 1831.

Today the river is as busy as ever. It is still possible to hire rowing boats, almost identical in style to those used three hundred years ago. Walking and cycling along the towpath is very popular and in the summer the riverside is heaving with revellers. Concerts are arranged in August, swelling numbers still more. The quays are still there and pleasure boats ferry passengers up- and downstream. The river has a timeless quality and remains one of the highlights of the town, appealing to residents and visitors alike.

LEFT, TOP Do not disturb!

LEFT, BOTTOM AND OPPOSITE
Some more alert local
fishermen: grebe,
cormorant and heron.

The high tide reaches
the front entrance of the
White Cross pub and
customers have to come
and go by the side door –
or paddle!

bridges

As Richmond grew in size it became more obvious that a bridge was needed to join St Margaret's and Twickenham to the town. In 1772 the construction of a wooden bridge was proposed. Many arguments raged about its exact location and building didn't actually start until 1774, by which time it had been decided to build a stone bridge. This took three years to complete.

The new bridge was a tontine bridge, so named after Lorenzo Tonti, a Neapolitan banker who had initiated the building of the first tontine bridge in France around 1650. His idea worked as follows. A group of subscribers paid to have the bridge built privately and they owned it. Each subscriber nominated one person to receive an annual dividend from any profits made. The bridge was subject to a toll, the original fee set at the same sum as the ferry. This dividend would continue for as long as the nominee lived. Once the nominee had died the profits would be shared amongst the surviving nominees. Eventually one nominee would enjoy the whole income. On the demise of the last nominee the bridge would become free to cross.

The subscribers' dilemma was who to choose as their nominee. Obviously, nominating an infant would mean that the dividends would keep coming for longer, but infant mortality rates in the eighteenth century were very high. Girls were slightly less likely to die than boys, but when they grew up they had to confront the dangers of childbirth. If they managed that hurdle, women tended to live longer than men.

The final tontine holder died aged eighty-six in 1859. It was a woman who must have been twelve months old when her parents nominated her. She was the sole beneficiary for the last five and a half years of her life and died a wealthy woman. The people of Richmond must have been relieved when she popped off and it became free to cross the river.

In 1831 London Bridge was rebuilt and the embankment of the river improved so that tidal water flowed more quickly in and out of the capital. This had a devastating effect in Richmond, where the Thames was reduced to a trickle at low tide. It was even possible to play a cricket match on the riverbed at Twickenham. Many resolutions of this problem were discussed and after much pontificating it was finally decided to build a new lock and weir with a footbridge across the river from Old Deer Park to St Margaret's. The lock was opened in 1894 and its sluice gates control the flow of tidal water.

In 1846 the railway reached Richmond. This proved extremely popular and it was decided to extend the line first to Twickenham and then to Staines, Datchet and, in 1849, to Windsor. The railway bridge was built across the river in 1848.

By the beginning of the last century cars were becoming increasingly widespread and the small road bridge became inadequate for the level of traffic. A new main road to London, the Great Chertsey Road, was constructed and the project involved the building of a new bridge. The Twickenham road bridge was opened by the then Prince of Wales in 1933.

BOATS and BICYCLES for HIRE

Richmond Bridge, with Richmond Hill visible in the distance.

Fresh, locally grown produce.

A stallholder at the
farmers' market.

music

Whenever royalty came to Richmond, entertainers were not far behind. The strolling minstrels who played to the court were later followed by more formal groups of musicians. Henry VIII himself was apparently very accomplished on several instruments and composed his own music, the famous 'Greensleeves' being attributed to him. During the puritanical years of the Commonwealth court activities at Richmond were suspended, but after the accession of Charles II there was a renewed demand for public concerts and performances by talented professional musicians.

In the eighteenth century the London music season lasted from October to May. During the summer months the musicians toured the spa towns, which had become popular resorts. Conveniently for Richmond, just as there was a lull in royal activity in the town a spring was discovered that exuded Epsom-like water, thought to be good for the spirit.

An entrepreneur of the time invested in Richmond Wells, building an assembly room and pump room and landscaping gardens on the site of the present-day Poppy Factory. The area reached the height of its popularity in the 1750s. It was hugely fashionable in summer, with visitors either coming for the day or renting a house for the season. Elegant ladies and gentlemen took the waters and were entertained by daily concerts, enjoying gala nights on Mondays and Thursdays.

Towards the end of the century Richmond Wells became rather rowdy, with a raffish set of young male drinkers and gamblers moving in. They attracted women of disrepute and the whole place went downhill fast, becoming rather sleazy. The establishment of the new theatre on the green in 1765 may have hastened the deterioration of the area, providing a

Musical performances held outdoors in spring and summer are one of the joys of Richmond.

rival musical venue and possibly leading to the gambling set taking over from the more refined theatre goers at Richmond Wells. By 1763 Susanna and Rebecca Houblon, two spinsters of the parish who lived opposite this scene of debauchery, had had enough. They bought the site for £400 and closed it down, much to the relief of many townspeople.

Richmond continued to attract composers and performers. Johann Christian Bach was music master to Queen Charlotte, wife of George III, and lived in Richmond, practising regularly with other court musicians in a house on Kew Green. In 1846 the Ethiopian Serenaders arrived, the forerunners of a group who were later to put on Black and White Minstrel Shows. Gustav Holst, best known as the composer of *The Planets*, was a music teacher at St Paul's Girls' School in Hammersmith and between 1904 and 1908 lived in Richmond at 31 Gena Road.

A revolution in music took place in Richmond during the 1960s. While Liverpool's Cavern Club was spawning the British Beat Boom, the suburbs of southwest London were thumping out the grittier sound of rhythm and blues. In 1961 the first National Jazz Festival took place in Richmond. In later years afternoon sessions were reserved for jazz acts, but the evening sessions would also feature rhythm and blues bands made popular at the two local, rival clubs – Eel Pie Island and the Crawdaddy Club.

In 1963 a jazz writer and impresario started a rhythm and blues night at the Station Hotel, now Edward's Bar. An unknown band called the Rolling Stones became the resident Sunday-night entertainment. Their popularity grew and grew as word got round about how good they were. One night they performed a particularly rousing version of

the 'Crawdaddy Blues' – and the Crawdaddy Club was born. The club soon had to move to Richmond Athletic Ground to accommodate the crowds.

The Stones moved on to bigger and better venues and another band, led by an ex-student of Kingston Art College, Eric Clapton, took over the Sunday-night slot. The Yardbirds were initially booed, but guitar heroes Jeff Beck and Jimmy Page (later of Led Zeppelin) went on to play lead guitar for them. Over at Eel Pie Island, John Mayall and his Bluesbreakers, featuring Eric Clapton and Peter Green (later of Fleetwood Mac), Long John Baldry's Hoochie Coochie Men, featuring Rod Stewart, and The Who were all strutting their stuff. Pete Townshend and Mick Jagger still live in Richmond, and Peter Green lived there under his real name, Peter Greenbaum, during his reclusive years.

Who would have thought that sleepy, suburban, middle-class Richmond would have given birth to some of the greatest rock musicians of the last century?

Cricket has been played on the green since the seventeenth century and matches are still held there every week in summer. Afterwards, refreshments are available in the Cricketers pub, which has been serving fans and players for over three hundred years.

pubs

Richmond has always had more public drinking houses than is usual for a town of its size. This is presumably because in the early years the royal entourages that descended on the town had to be fed, watered and housed. Later, summer visitors filled the coffers of the victuallers and today the place is constantly full of tourists and other out-of-town visitors coming for a drink or two.

Although drinking is talked about as a modern-day problem, it has been the scourge of many a past generation as well. In the thirteenth century London was notorious for 'the immoderate drinking of the foolish', with the rich consuming wines from the Rhineland, Burgundy, Madeira and the Iberian peninsula and the poor being more partial to ale and beer. A good idea of the debauchery of medieval times can be gleaned from Chaucer's account of contemporary life in *The Canterbury Tales*.

Excessive drinking led to the introduction of an excise tax on beer in 1643, but if drinking had been a problem in the past it became a nightmare in the eighteenth century, when the habit reached massive – even crisis – proportions. Samuel Johnson declared 'a man is never happy in the present unless he is drunk'. A vast number of his fellow citizens seemed to agree.

The big problem was gin, which is said to have been brought to England from Holland by William III. It was taxed more lightly than beer and could be sold without a licence; as a result it was available everywhere and apparently you could be 'drunk for a penny, dead drunk for two pence'. The demon of London for half a century, gin was held responsible for the deaths of thousands of men, women and children. A combination of gin shop closures and tax

OPPOSITE A summer's evening presents the perfect opportunity to put your feet up and have a drink by the river.

BELOW, LEFT A sign points to the side door of the White Cross pub, which is the only accessible entrance at high tide.

BELOW, RIGHT Drinkers take their pick from many riverside bars and cosy pubs like the Roebuck, one of the oldest public houses in Richmond.

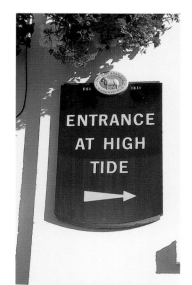

increases had quelled the frenzy by the middle of the eighteenth century.

Of the pubs recorded in Richmond in a 1724 survey of licensed properties, many still exist on the same site, although all have been through some degree of refurbishment and many have changed their names. The Black Horse, on the corner of Sheen Road and Queens Road, was originally a posting inn and dates from 1718. The Roebuck, on the top of Richmond Hill, and the Angel and Crown in Church Court (probably the oldest of the three) were also mentioned in the survey. All three retain their original name and site.

The Orange Tree has been around since 1720 but has moved very slightly, the pub being in its present position since 1898. The Cricketers on the green – originally the Crickett Players – was opened in 1741 and rebuilt in 1844 after being destroyed by a fire. It has always been associated with the cricket teams whose home ground is the green. The White Cross has been in its riverside situation since 1740, although it was rebuilt in the 1830s. It is on the site of the old Carthusian Monastery, home of the monks belonging to the order of the White Cross (co-incidentally, it was once owned by a man named Cross). On the corner opposite the Odeon cinema, there used to be a pub called the Plough. This was the oldest known establishment in Richmond, dating back to 1657. It seems that these days it is renamed and refurbished every two or three years, but it is obviously a prime site for drawing in the customers.

The Beer Act of 1830 allowed beer to be sold by any householder who paid a two-guinea excise fee. Intended to discourage the consumption of gin, the Act led to a rise in the number of beer houses. In 1830, before the Beer Act, there were twenty-nine pubs in Richmond; by 1880 there were seventy-three. About a quarter of those remain open for business today.

ABOVE The Terrace, at the top of Richmond Hill.

OPPOSITE, TOP Richmond Green early one summer's morning.

OPPOSITE, BOTTOM The observatory, visible from the Old Deer Park.

autumn

PREVIOUS PAGE Leaves redden above the statue of Old Father Thames.

LEFT The arch under the railway bridge.

RIGHT, TOP Shafts of light by the gate near the towpath at Petersham.

RIGHT, BOTTOM Out for an autumnal stroll along the towpath.

The ha-ha between the towpath and the Old Deer Park, dug by Farmer George to keep his cattle from straying.

Leaves carpet the
towpath near the lock
and the bridge leading to
the Old Deer Park.

rugby

'I remember him perfectly. He was generally regarded as inclined to take advantages at football.' This is how the Reverend Thomas Harris, a fellow ex-pupil of Rugby School, described William Webb Ellis's habit of cheating at football. Picking up the ball and running with it, he created the new game of rugby – or so the story goes. A rudimentary set of rules to the embryonic game were draughted at Rugby School in 1845.

Rugby has always played a large role in the life of Richmond, with Richmond, London Welsh, London Scottish, Rosslyn Park and Harlequins all senior sides playing locally on Saturdays. On days when internationals are played at Twickenham, the town is full of supporters and the England team regularly stays at the Petersham Hotel on the hill.

Formed in 1861, Richmond Rugby Club is one of the oldest clubs in the country. Originally they played on Richmond Green, later moving first to the Old Deer Park and then to the Athletic Ground, where they still play today. The first-ever club fixture was played between Richmond and Blackheath in 1864. The first floodlit match was played on Richmond's ground in 1878.

The secretary of Richmond Club, Edwin Ash, was one of the men who over a long lunch in a London restaurant in 1871 founded the Rugby Football Union (RFU), becoming its first secretary. In 1996 Richmond became the first professional rugby club in the UK. This was a short-lived venture, however, since the financial backer pulled out three years later, leaving the club bankrupt and in administration. The professional squad was disbanded and the amateur club was demoted eight leagues as punishment. They have

subsequently gone on to win their league and gain promotion in each of the last four seasons. In doing so they have, at the time of writing, set a world record of seventy-nine consecutive league wins.

A new company now runs the club. Richmond Vikings Ltd was formed to rescue the club after all the turmoil of the late nineties. They bought back the rights to the club name and its share of the lease of the Athletic Ground, which nearly became the property of Chelsea Football Club a few years ago. Richmond share the ground with London Scottish, an exiles' club formed in 1878 that has provided more international players and more Lions captains than any other club side in Britain.

During the early years of rugby, internationals were played all over the country. One of the grounds regularly used was Richmond's. As the game grew it was decided that a national stadium was required. Eventually the RFU purchased, for the grand sum of £5,572 12s 6d, an area of 10¼ acres on the site of an old market garden. Affectionately known as the 'Cabbage Patch', this became the hallowed turf of Twickenham. The first match to be played there was between Richmond and Harlequins in 1909. The first international, between England and Wales, took place a year later. Today's magnificent stadium holds 70,000 fans and the victorious England side returned there in 2003 to parade their newly won World Cup.

**LEFT, TOP** Hips and a horse.

LEFT, BOTTOM The tunnel of hawthorn leading to Petersham Meadow.

RIGHT Town or country? Cows graze on Petersham Meadow.

The view from Richmond Hill, with the Thames a sheet of silver under autumn skies.

the poppy factory

Richmond's cinema, station and Poppy Factory are all excellent examples of Art Deco architecture.

After the First World War a great wave of remembrance, gratitude and sympathy swept through the nation; remembrance of the fallen, gratitude to the men and women who fought and sympathy for the disabled. War memorials sprang up in every town and village across the land.

The poppy was first worn as a symbol of remembrance by an American woman by the name of Miss Moina Michael. She had read a poem called 'In Flanders Fields', written by a Canadian Professor of Medicine, Colonel John McCrae, who served and died in France during the war. In his poem he wrote:

> In Flanders fields the poppies blow
> Between the crosses, row on row,
> That mark our place . . .

This poem so moved her that she vowed always to wear a poppy as a mark of respect. She worked in a YMCA in New York and through this establishment met a French woman called Mme Guérin, who was intrigued by the symbol of the poppy. Mme Guérin heard her story and conceived the idea of turning poppies to a practical use. She travelled the world to publicize her project of making the poppy an international sign of remembrance. She enlisted French women and children from the places most devastated by the war to produce the poppies, hoping to help local regeneration. The public response to the first poppy day in 1921 was so overwhelming that the British Legion decided to seek a source of the emblem in the home artificial-flower trade.

In 1922, Major Howson, an ex-infantry officer and winner of the Military Cross, founded the Disabled Society, a charity that raised money for the most disabled as well as publishing a booklet called *Handbook for the Limbless* and, with other charities, lobbying for better artificial limbs. Major Howson realized that what the disabled wanted more than anything else was employment and to earn their own living. The British Legion gave the Disabled Society a grant to set up a poppy-making enterprise. A room in the Old Kent Road provided employment for five disabled ex-servicemen and the Poppy Factory was born.

Sales of poppies grew and in 1926 the Poppy Factory was moved to a larger site in Richmond. At the same time the Cardigan House Estate (on the site of the old Richmond Wells) was purchased, to provide housing for the men working at the factory. By 1934, 30 million poppies were being sold annually and 360 men were employed.

Today, the factory still produces all the world's remembrance poppies. It continues to employ disabled ex-servicemen and women or their disabled relatives, and to provide housing for the employees.

ABOVE, LEFT The Terrace, at the top of Richmond Hill, on a beautiful autumn day.

ABOVE, RIGHT The Petersham Hotel, seen from The Terrace.

the park

Charles I loved hunting and although he already had land at Hampton Court and James I's New Park to roam in, he coveted the gravel uplands that today are the site of Richmond Park. He began to enclose the area with a brick wall and by 1637 the building works were completed. They made the king very unpopular locally as he took much privately owned land – with or without the owners' consent – to ensure that the park had a regular shape. After Charles' execution in 1649 the Commonwealth government gave the park to the City of London, in thanks for their support during the Civil War. The Corporation of London restored it to the monarchy when Charles II acceded to the throne and it remains a Royal Park today.

Today Richmond Park is still a place of recreation but the deer are no longer hunted. There are about 650 deer in the park: 375 fallow deer and 275 red deer. During the rut in autumn there is a lot of activity among the stags; they rush around, often with bracken in their antlers, bellowing and posturing and occasionally fighting for the right to mate with the females. It is exciting to watch but visitors should keep their distance, as the animals are highly charged at this time and potentially dangerous to anyone who gets in their way. The other time of year to be careful is in June and July, when the young are born and the females become quite aggressive about protecting their offspring. Many a dog owner has been chased by an angry doe during this period.

Originally a molecatcher's cottage (molecatchers were employed to clear molehills from the path of huntsmen) and later the home of philosopher and pacifist Bertrand Russell, the imposing Pembroke Lodge is now a very busy café. It is also possible to be married there and hold the wedding reception in function rooms with wonderful views of the Thames.

The gardens of the lodge are formally laid out, with a rose garden and a laburnum tunnel. At the Richmond Gate end of the gardens is Henry VIII's mound, on the site of a prehistoric barrow or burial ground. From here it is possible to view St Paul's Cathedral. In 1710 an avenue of trees was planted from the mound, the highest point in the park, towards the newly built cathedral. A hundred years later Sidmouth Wood was planted and to retain the view a landscaped 'drift way' had to be created through the wood. During the 1940s, when many gardeners were away at war, the view vanished, obliterated by the rampant undergrowth. In 1976, a local man, James Batten, rediscovered the vista and managed to restore it to its former glory. It is a magnificent sight on a clear day, a ten-mile pathway with the dome of St Paul's at the end.

Another old building in the park is White Lodge, the grand house built for George II in 1727. The king commissioned the design from Roger Morris and the Earl of Pembroke, who were also responsible for Marble Hill House in Twickenham. George III used White Lodge as a hunting box and Henry Addington, later Viscount Sidmouth, lived there after his short stint as Prime Minister. He became one of the greatest of Richmond Park's managers, carrying out extensive tree planting that has shaped the park of today. White Lodge is now the home of the Royal Ballet School. The best view of it is from Queen's Ride, the avenue often used by George III's consort, Queen Caroline, to reach the house.

In spring the park's big attraction is the Isabella Plantation, first enclosed in 1831. In 1920 Ernest Wilson, a

ABOVE A red stag bellows during the autumn rut.

BELOW Silver birch trees in Richmond Park.

famous plant collector responsible for introducing many azaleas into Britain, set up the National Collection of Kuzume Azaleas in the plantation. The site was further developed in the late 1940s, when it was transformed from a simple streamside walk to a spectacular woodland garden with glades, streams, ponds, heather and bogs. This reinvention of the area was down to George Thompson, park superintendent at the time, and Wally Miller, his head gardener. The Isabella Plantation was opened as a woodland garden in 1953.

There is a flat area of park by Roehampton Gate that is used by rugby players and an increasing number of kite fliers, and a golf course is situated between Roehampton Gate and Robin Hood Gate. At the car park near the golf club it is possible to hire bicycles and there is a dedicated cycle path that runs around the circumference of the park.

All in all Richmond Park is a fabulous space – a great legacy from an arrogant king who enclosed the park for his own selfish reasons but ended up by benefiting the whole community.

OPPOSITE, TOP Gulls
line up on posts in
Terrace Gardens.

OPPOSITE, BOTTOM
A deserted Richmond
Green in autumn sunshine.

BELOW Looking down
to the river in Terrace
Gardens.

theatres

Travelling troupes of actors accompanied the royal household as it toured the country, moving from one royal establishment to another. During the fourteenth century Chaucer came to Richmond with Richard II, and later he was followed by England's greatest playwright, William Shakespeare. There are many records of Shakespeare's troupe performing for Elizabeth I at Richmond Palace and it is said that he stayed with a friend at 1 The Green when in town.

Up until the eighteenth century there was no dedicated venue in which the actors performed. The first theatre to be purpose built was opened by Will Penkerton, a comedian who specialized in knock-about farce. He converted a barn on Richmond Hill into a simple theatre in 1719 and put on plays there until his death in 1725.

On the corner of the green at the top of Old Palace Lane, the first theatre of note in Richmond was erected for an actor, James Love, and was probably designed by his father and brother, who were both architects. The design, which included features such as dark panelling in the auditorium to focus the audience's attention on the stage, aroused widespread interest and was copied elsewhere, including at Bristol Theatre which today is the oldest continuously used theatre in the country. David Garrick, a fellow actor and friend of Love's, wrote a special prologue for the opening night. George III and Queen Charlotte became patrons and the theatre was later expanded because of its popularity.

Edmund Kean, one of the most famous actors of the time, acted regularly at Richmond Theatre and drew large audiences from London as well as local crowds. It was a hazardous journey for ardent theatregoers coming from the city to see their heroes perform. Coaches had to pass through much wooded and wild land on the way to the refinement of Richmond and there was a danger that travellers would be accosted by highwaymen and robbed of their jewels and money. The management of the theatre advised patrons that a number of armed guards were employed to patrol the roads along the route.

Like many famous actors Edmond Kean was something of a prima donna. One night the audience had the cheek to applaud the rest of the cast as much as they did its star. Kean was outraged and he wrote to the manager saying, 'I have the greatest respect for you and the best wishes for your professional success but if I play Richmond again I'll be damned.' He did, however, play Richmond again. In fact, he ended up buying a share in the theatre, living and eventually dying in Richmond and is buried in the local churchyard. Kean's funeral was quite an occasion. The shops in George Street were closed and twenty townsmen sworn in as special constables to help with crowd control. During the service some wag in the congregation apparently shouted, 'Bravo, Teddy, you've drawn a full house at last!'

This theatre was eventually shut down and demolished in 1884. Its demise was partly caused by the coming of the railways, which increased the ease with which locals could get up to London to see a West End production. However, a rich hotelier named Monflet decided that Richmond did need a purpose-built theatre of its own. In 1889 he acquired a site next to the library and commissioned Frank Matcham, a leading architect of the day, to design the building. Richmond Theatre still thrives today, a testing ground for plays that if

successful later transfer to the West End. Many famous actors, from Charlie Chaplin and Stan Laurel to the great Shakespearean actors Olivier, Gielgud and Richardson, as well as the more bizarre Phil Silvers and Les Dawson, have performed there. Dame Anna Neagle appeared in the longest-ever run – the pantomime *Cinderella* in 1982. The theatre was refurbished in 1991 at a cost of £3.5 million and is now a Grade 2 listed building.

There is also a famous fringe theatre in Richmond, which started life in the upper room of the Orange Tree pub. Because of its popularity and success it moved in 1991 into larger premises across the road, where it continues to flourish.

LEFT, TOP The Royal Star & Garter Home, looking down over the cows in Petersham Meadow.

LEFT, BOTTOM Flats built on the site of the old ice rink. Richmond is still waiting for a replacement rink.

RIGHT, TOP Trumpeters' House, built in the early eighteenth century on part of the site formerly occupied by Richmond Palace.

RIGHT, BOTTOM The wonderful architecture of Cholmondeley Walk.

Richmond lock at dusk.

The station at night.

Sunset from the top of
Richmond Hill.

index

Illustration captions in italics

almshouses 48
American University 27, *27*
Angel and Crown pub 81
Anne of Bohemia 7, 10, 11
Anne of Cleves 40
Arcadia Initiative 15
architecture 22, *22*, *25*, *27*, *27*,
  53, *53*, *106*
Asgill House *53*
Ash, Edwin 91

Bach, Johann Christian 77
Batten, James 100
Black Horse pub 81
Boleyn, Anne 40
Brewers' Lane *53*
British Legion 97

Carmelite monastery 10
Caroline of Ansbach 53
Carthusian monastery 11, 81
Catherine of Aragon 40
Charles I 41, 100
Charles II 48, 76
Charlotte Sophia of Mecklenburg-
  Strelitz 53–4, 77, 100, 104
Chaucer, Geoffrey 11,
  80, 104
Cholmondeley Walk *11*, 65, *106*
Clapton, Eric 77
Colet, Dean 53
Crawdaddy Club 77
cricket 22, *78*
Cricketers pub 22, *78*, 81

Dickens, Charles 44
Disabled Society 97

Doggett's Coat and Badge
  Race 62
Downe House 15
Duppa, Bishop 48

Edward I 10, 22
Edward II 10
Edward III, the Confessor
  7, 10
Edward VI 40
Eel Pie Island 77
Eleanor of Castile 22
Elizabeth I 22, 40, *40*, 62, 104
Elizabeth II 45
Ellecker House 27

farmers' market *75*
First World War 97
Fitzherbert, Mrs *53*, 54
frost fairs 65

Gainsborough, Thomas 15
Garrick, David 104
George I 53
George II 53
George III 53, 54, *88*, 100, 104
George IV 44
George Street 27, *40*, 54, 104
Gothic House 27
Great River Race *62*
Green, Peter 77
Guérin, Mme 97

Hampton Court 40
Harlequins Rugby Club 91
Henry I 10
Henry V 11
Henry VII 7, 11, 40, *40*
Henry VIII 22, 40, 62,

76, 100
Herschel 54
Hickey, William 48
Hill Rise *46*
Holst, Gustav 77
Houblon, Rebecca 48, 77
Howson, Major 97

Isabella of France 10
Isabella Plantation *35*, 100–101

James I 41, 100
Johnson, Samuel 80

Kean, Edmund 104
Kew 53, 54
Kingston 10

London Scottish Rugby Club 91
London Welsh Rugby Club 91, *91*
Love, James 104

McCrae, Colonel John
Maids of Honour Row 27, 53, *54*,
Marble Hill House 53, 100
Marshgate House 27, *53*
Matcham, Frank 104
May Fair 22, *56*
Mayall, John 77
Michael, Moina 97
Michel, Humphrey 48
Miller, Wally 100
Mortimer, Roger 10

Nightingale Lane 15

Old Deer Park *12*, *19*, *49*, 53, *82*
Old Palace Lane 27, 104
Old Palace Terrace *27*

Orange Tree pub 81, *91*, 105
Ormonde, Earl of 53

Palladio, Andrea 27
Paston, Sir Robert 22
Paved Court *29*
Pembroke Lodge 100
Pembroke Villas *22*, *25*, 27
Penkerton, Will 104
Petersham Hotel *15*, 91, *98*
Petersham Meadow *15*, *92*, *106*
Poppy Factory 27, 76, 97, *97*
Portland Terrace *22*, 27
pubs 80–81
Purcell, Henry 15

Queen's Ride *30*, 100

railways 7, 70
Reynolds, Sir Joshua 15
Richard II 10, 11, 104
Richard III 40
Richmond Bridge 65, 70, *70*, *73*
Richmond Green 22, *25*, *82*, *103*
Richmond Hill 15, *15*, *17*, 41,
  73, *95*, *110*
Richmond Lodge 53
Richmond Palace 40–41, *40*
Richmond Park *31*, *60*, 100–101
Richmond Rugby Club 91
Richmond Theatre 104–105, *105*
Richmond Wells 76–7
Roebuck pub 15, *81*
Rolling Stones 77
Rosslyn Park Rugby Club 91
Royal Mid-Surrey golf course 11,
  53, 54
Royal Star & Garter Home
  44–5, *45*, *106*

rugby 91
Russell, Bertrand 100

St Paul's Cathedral 100
Seymour, Jane 40
Shakespeare, William 40, 104
Shene 7, 10–11, 40
Sheridan, Richard 15
Sidmouth, Viscount 100
swan upping 65

Terrace, The 15, *53*, 54, *82*, *98*
Terrace Gardens *11*, *21*, 27,
  37, *65*, *103*
Terry, Quinlan 27
theatres 104–5
Thompson, George 100
Thomson, James 15
Tonti, Lorenzo 70
Townshend, Pete 77
Trumpeters' House *106*
Turner, J.M.W. 15

Walpole, Horace 27
Walpole, Sir Robert 53
Webb Ellis, William 91
White Cross pub 62, *69*, 81
White Lodge 100
Wick House 15, 27
William III 80
Wilson, Ernest 100–101
Wolsey, Cardinal 40
Wordsworth, William 15
Wright, Sir George 48

Yardbirds 77